Microwave Cooking: Microwave ovens vary in wattage. Use the cooking times as guidelines and check for doneness before adding more time.

Nutritional Analysis: Every effort has been made to check the accuracy of the nutritional information that appears with each recipe. However, because numerous variables account for a wide range of values for certain foods, nutritive analyses in this book should be considered approximate.

INDEX

ENJOY YOUR AIR FRYER

Do you love fried foods but try to avoid them? You no longer need to worry.

The air fryer is your answer to preparing fried foods without the extra calories, fat, or mess in the kitchen. You'll get the taste and texture of fried foods—crispy, tasty, and crunchy—that you love and crave, without the added guilt often felt when consuming them. Plus, you'll soon see how your air fryer is so easy to use, cooks food faster, and provides a no-fuss clean up.

You'll love the ability to prepare fried foods in your air fryer, but you'll also soon find that you can prepare all types of other foods, too. Make everything from appetizers to meals to sides and even desserts! You can bake in it, grill in it, steam in it, roast in it, and reheat in it.

Choose from more than 80 ideas here, or create your own.

Now get started and have fun eating and serving all those healthier foods without the added guilt.

HELPFUL HINTS

- Read the air fryer's manufacturer's directions carefully before cooking to make sure you understand the specific features of your air fryer before starting to cook.

- Preheat your air fryer for 2 to 3 minutes before cooking.

- You can cook foods typically cooked in the oven in your air fryer. But because the air fryer is more condensed than a regular oven, it is recommended that recipes cut 25°F to 50°F off the temperature and 20% off the typical cooking times.

- Avoid having foods stick to your air fryer basket by using nonstick cooking spray or cooking on parchment paper or foil. You can also get food to brown and crisp more easily by spraying occasionally with nonstick cooking spray during the cooking process.

- Don't overfill your basket. Each air fryer differs in its basket size. Cook foods in batches as needed.

- Use toothpicks to hold food in place. You may notice that light foods may blow around from the pressure of the fan. Just be sure to secure foods in the basket to prevent this.

- Check foods while cooking by opening the air fryer basket. This will not disturb cooking times. Once you return the basket, the cooking resumes.

- Experiment with cooking times of various foods. Test foods for doneness before consuming—check meats and poultry with a meat thermometer, and use a toothpick to test muffins and cupcakes.

- Use your air fryer to cook frozen foods, too! Frozen French fries, fish sticks, chicken nuggets, individual pizzas—these all work great. Just remember to reduce cooking temperatures and times.

ESTIMATED COOKING TEMPERATURES/TIMES*

FOOD	TEMPERATURE	TIMING
Vegetables (asparagus, broccoli, corn-on-cob, green beans, mushrooms, cherry tomatoes)	390°F	5 to 6 min.
Vegetables (bell peppers, cauliflower, eggplant, onions, potatoes, zucchini)	390°F	8 to 12 min.
Chicken (bone-in)	370°F	20 to 25 min.
Chicken (boneless)	370°F	12 to 15 min.
Beef (ground beef)	370°F	15 to 17 min.
Beef (steaks, roasts)	390°F	10 to 15 min.
Pork	370°F	12 to 15 min.
Fish	390°F	10 to 12 min.
Frozen Foods	390°F	10 to 15 min.

*This is just a guide. All food varies in size, weight, and texture. Be sure to test your food for preferred doneness before consuming it. Also, some foods will need to be shaken or flipped to help distribute ingredients for proper cooking.

Make note of the temperatures and times that work best for you for continued success of your air fryer.

Enjoy and have fun!

**QUICK JELLY-FILLED
BISCUIT DOUGHNUT BALLS**
(page 12)

CHAPTER 1

BREAKFAST BITES

FRENCH TOAST STICKS

MAKES 4 SERVINGS

4 eggs

⅓ cup reduced-fat
(2%) milk

1 teaspoon ground
cinnamon

1 teaspoon vanilla

4 slices Italian bread,
cut into 3 portions
each

1 teaspoon powdered
sugar

¼ cup maple syrup

1. Combine eggs, milk, cinnamon and vanilla in large bowl.

2. Dip bread sticks in egg mixture to coat.

3. Preheat air fryer to 370°F. Line basket with parchment paper; spray with nonstick cooking spray.

4. Cook in batches 8 to 10 minutes or until golden brown. Dust lightly with powdered sugar; serve with maple syrup.

Calories 230, **Total Fat** 6g, **Saturated Fat** 2g, **Cholesterol** 190mg, **Sodium** 250mg, **Carbohydrates** 31g, **Dietary Fiber** 0g, **Protein** 10g

BREAKFAST FLATS

MAKES 4 SERVINGS

1 package (14 ounces) refrigerated pizza dough

All-purpose flour, for dusting

1½ cups (6 ounces) shredded medium Cheddar cheese

8 slices bacon, cooked crisp and diced (optional)

4 eggs, fried

Kosher salt and black pepper (optional)

1. Preheat air fryer to 370°F. Line basket with parchment paper.

2. Divide pizza dough into 4 equal portions. Roll out on lightly floured surface into rectangles roughly 8½×4 inches. Top each evenly with cheese and bacon, if desired. Cook in batches 5 to 7 minutes or until crust is golden brown and crisp and cheese is melted.

3. Top baked flats with fried egg; season with salt and pepper, if desired. Serve warm.

Calories 290, **Total Fat** 11g, **Saturated Fat** 5g, **Cholesterol** 200mg, **Sodium** 630mg, **Carbohydrates** 32g, **Dietary Fiber** 0g, **Protein** 14g

QUICK JELLY-FILLED BISCUIT DOUGHNUT BALLS

MAKES 20 DOUGHNUT BALLS

1 package (about 7 ounces) refrigerated reduced-fat biscuit dough (10 biscuits)

¼ cup coarse sugar

1 cup strawberry preserves*

*If preserves are very chunky, process in food processor 10 seconds or press through fine-mesh sieve.

1. Preheat air fryer to 370°F.

2. Separate biscuits into 10 portions. Cut each in half; roll dough into balls to create 20 balls.

3. Cook in batches 5 to 6 minutes or until golden brown.

4. Place sugar in large bowl. Coat warm balls in sugar. Let cool. Using a piping bag with medium star tip; fill bag with preserves. Poke hole in side of each doughnut ball with paring knife; fill with preserves. Serve immediately.

Calories 80, **Total Fat** 1g, **Saturated Fat** 0g, **Cholesterol** 0mg, **Sodium** 80mg, **Carbohydrates** 17g, **Dietary Fiber** 0g, **Protein** 1g

RASPBERRY PUFFS

MAKES 8 PUFFS

1 package (8 ounces) refrigerated crescent roll dough

¼ cup raspberry fruit spread

½ of an 8-ounce package cream cheese, softened

1 to 2 teaspoons sugar

2 tablespoons reduced-fat (2%) milk

¼ teaspoon vanilla

1. Preheat air fryer to 370°F. Line basket with parchment paper.

2. Separate crescent roll dough into 8 triangles; unroll on lightly floured surface. Brush 1½ teaspoons fruit spread evenly over each roll. Roll up each triangle, starting at wide end.

3. Cook in batches 5 to 6 minutes or until lightly golden. Cool.

4. Meanwhile, whisk together cream cheese, sugar, milk and vanilla in small bowl until smooth. Spoon about 1 tablespoon cream cheese mixture over each cooled roll or serve on the side, as desired.

VARIATION: For an even lighter-tasting roll, replace the cream cheese mixture with powdered sugar. Simply sprinkle 2 tablespoons evenly over all.

Calories 127, **Total Fat** 6g, **Saturated Fat** 2g, **Cholesterol** 6mg, **Sodium** 223mg, **Carbohydrates** 16g, **Dietary Fiber** 0g, **Protein** 3g

BREAKFAST BURRITOS

MAKES 4 SERVINGS

4 turkey breakfast
   sausage links

2 eggs

½ teaspoon ground
   cumin (optional)

4 (6-inch) yellow or
   white corn tortillas

¼ cup salsa

1. Preheat air fryer to 370°F. Line basket with parchment paper.

2. Cook sausages 6 to 8 minutes or until browned on the outside and cooked through, shaking occasionally during cooking. Remove sausages to plate.

3. Whisk eggs and cumin, if desired, in small bowl. Heat small skillet over medium-high heat. Cook eggs until done.

4. Place sausage link in middle of each tortilla. Spoon equal amounts of scrambled egg on top of sausage. Roll up to enclose the filling; secure with toothpick.

5. Cook in air fryer 3 to 5 minutes or until heated through.

6. Pour salsa in small bowl. Serve with burritos.

Calories 130, **Total Fat** 5g, **Saturated Fat** 1.5g, **Cholesterol** 110mg, **Sodium** 300mg, **Carbohydrates** 12g, **Dietary Fiber** 1.5g, **Protein** 9g

CRUNCHY FRENCH TOAST STICKS

MAKES 6 SERVINGS

6 slices Italian bread (each 1 inch thick, about 3½ to 4 inches in diameter)

4 cups cornflakes, crushed

3 eggs

⅔ cup reduced-fat (2%) milk

1 tablespoon sugar

1 teaspoon vanilla

1 teaspoon ground cinnamon, plus additional for serving

¼ teaspoon ground nutmeg

1 container (6 ounces) vanilla yogurt

¼ cup maple syrup

1. Preheat air fryer to 370°F. Line basket with parchment paper. Remove crusts from bread, if desired. Cut each bread slice into three strips. Place cornflakes on waxed paper.

2. Whisk eggs, milk, sugar, vanilla, 1 teaspoon cinnamon and nutmeg in shallow bowl. Dip bread strips in egg mixture, turning to generously coat all sides. Roll in cornflakes, coating all sides.

3. Cook in batches 8 to 10 minutes, turning halfway through cooking, or until golden brown.

4. Meanwhile, combine yogurt and maple syrup in small bowl. Sprinkle with additional cinnamon, if desired. Serve French toast sticks with yogurt mixture.

Calories 270, **Total Fat** 4g, **Saturated Fat** 1g, **Cholesterol** 95mg, **Sodium** 360mg, **Carbohydrates** 47g, **Dietary Fiber** 0g, **Protein** 11g

FALAFEL NUGGETS
(page 26)

CHAPTER 2

NIBBLES & BITES

BAKED SPINACH BALLS

MAKES 24 BALLS (12 SERVINGS)

1 package (6 ounces)
   sage and onion
   or herb-seasoned
   bread stuffing mix

1 small onion, chopped

2 tablespoons grated
   Parmesan cheese

1 clove garlic, minced

¼ teaspoon dried
   thyme

¼ teaspoon black
   pepper

1 package (10 ounces)
   frozen chopped
   spinach, thawed
   and well drained

¼ cup chicken broth

2 egg whites, beaten

   Dijon or honey
   mustard (optional)

1. Combine stuffing mix, onion, cheese, garlic, thyme and pepper in medium bowl; mix well. Combine spinach, broth and egg whites in separate medium bowl; mix well. Stir into stuffing mixture. Cover; refrigerate 1 hour or until mixture is firm.

2. Preheat air fryer to 370°F.

3. Shape mixture into 24 balls. Cook in batches 5 minutes or until spinach balls are browned. Serve with mustard for dipping, if desired.

Calories 52, **Total Fat** 1g, **Saturated Fat** 1g, **Cholesterol** 1mg, **Sodium** 227mg, **Carbohydrates** 9g, **Dietary Fiber** 1g, **Protein** 3g

GREAT ZUKES PIZZA BITES

MAKES 16 BITES (8 SERVINGS)

1 medium zucchini

3 tablespoons pizza sauce

2 tablespoons tomato paste

¼ teaspoon dried oregano

¾ cup (3 ounces) shredded mozzarella cheese

¼ cup shredded Parmesan cheese

8 slices pitted black olives

8 slices pepperoni

1. Preheat air fryer to 400°F; spray basket with nonstick cooking spray.

2. Trim off and discard ends of zucchini. Cut zucchini into 16 (¼-inch-thick) diagonal slices.

3. Combine pizza sauce, tomato paste and oregano in small bowl; mix well. Spread scant teaspoon sauce over each zucchini slice. Combine cheeses in small bowl. Top each zucchini slice with 1 tablespoon cheese mixture, pressing down into sauce. Place 1 olive slice on each of 8 pizza bites. Place 1 folded pepperoni slice on each remaining pizza bite.

4. Cook in batches 1 to 2 minutes or until cheese is melted. Serve immediately.

Calories 75, **Total Fat** 5g, **Saturated Fat** 2g, **Cholesterol** 10mg, **Sodium** 288mg, **Carbohydrates** 3g, **Dietary Fiber** 1g, **Protein** 5g

FALAFEL NUGGETS

MAKES 12 SERVINGS

Sauce

2½ cups tomato sauce

⅓ cup tomato paste

2 tablespoons lemon juice

2 teaspoons sugar

1 teaspoon onion powder

½ teaspoon salt

Falafel

2 cans (about 15 ounces each) chickpeas, rinsed and drained

½ cup all-purpose flour

½ cup chopped fresh parsley

1 egg

¼ cup minced onion

3 tablespoons lemon juice

2 tablespoons minced garlic

2 teaspoons ground cumin

½ teaspoon salt

½ teaspoon ground red pepper or red pepper flakes

1. For sauce, combine tomato sauce, tomato paste, 2 tablespoons lemon juice, sugar, onion powder and ½ teaspoon salt in medium saucepan. Simmer over medium-low heat 20 minutes or until heated through. Cover and keep warm until ready to serve.

2. Preheat air fryer to 390°F. Line basket with foil; spray with nonstick cooking spray.

3. For falafel, combine chickpeas, flour, parsley, egg, minced onion, 3 tablespoons lemon juice, garlic, cumin, ½ teaspoon salt and ground red pepper in food processor or blender; process until well blended. Shape mixture into 1-inch balls. Spray with cooking spray.

4. Cook in batches 12 to 15 minutes, turning halfway through cooking, until browned. Serve with sauce.

Calories 120, **Total Fat** 2g, **Saturated Fat** 0g, **Cholesterol** 15mg, **Sodium** 660mg, **Carbohydrates** 20g, **Dietary Fiber** 5g, **Protein** 6g

BRIE BITES

MAKES 32 BITES (8 SERVINGS)

1 package (17¼ ounces) frozen puff pastry (2 sheets), thawed

¼ cup apricot preserves *or* red pepper jelly

1 round (8 ounces) Brie cheese, cut into 32 cubes

1. Preheat air fryer to 370°F.

2. Cut each pastry sheet into 16 squares.

3. Spread ½ teaspoon apricot preserves on each square. Place one cube Brie on one side of each square. Fold over opposite edge; use fork to seal edges completely.

4. Cook in batches 8 to 10 minutes or until pastry is golden brown.

Calories 160, **Total Fat** 11g, **Saturated Fat** 6g, **Cholesterol** 30mg, **Sodium** 230mg, **Carbohydrates** 10g, **Dietary Fiber** 0g, **Protein** 7g

HAPPY APPLE SALSA WITH CINNAMON PITA CHIPS

MAKES 3 SERVINGS

2 teaspoons sugar

¼ teaspoon ground cinnamon

2 pita bread rounds, split

1 tablespoon jelly or jam

1 medium apple, diced

1 tablespoon finely diced celery

1 tablespoon finely diced carrot

1 tablespoon golden raisins

1 teaspoon lemon juice

1. Preheat air fryer to 330°F.

2. Combine sugar and cinnamon in small bowl. Cut pita rounds into wedges. Spray with nonstick cooking spray; sprinkle with cinnamon-sugar.

3. Cook 8 to 10 minutes, shaking occasionally, until lightly browned. Set aside to cool.

4. Meanwhile, place jelly in medium microwavable bowl; microwave on HIGH 10 seconds. Stir in apple, celery, carrot, raisins and lemon juice. Serve salsa with pita chips.

Calories 130, **Total Fat** 0g, **Saturated Fat** 0g, **Cholesterol** 0mg, **Sodium** 160mg, **Carbohydrates** 30g, **Dietary Fiber** 1g, **Protein** 3g

THE BIG ONION

MAKES 6 SERVINGS

Dipping Sauce

½ cup light mayonnaise

2 tablespoons horseradish

1 tablespoon ketchup

¼ teaspoon paprika

⅛ teaspoon salt

⅛ teaspoon ground red pepper

⅛ teaspoon dried oregano

Onion

1 large sweet onion (about 1 pound)

½ cup all-purpose flour

1 tablespoon buttermilk

2 eggs

½ cup panko bread crumbs

1 tablespoon paprika

1½ teaspoons seafood seasoning

1. For sauce, combine mayonnaise, horseradish, ketchup, ¼ teaspoon paprika, salt, ground red pepper and oregano in small bowl; mix well. Cover and refrigerate until ready to serve.

2. For onion, cut about ½ inch off top of onion and peel off papery skin. Place onion cut side down on cutting board. Starting ½ inch from root, use large sharp knife to make one slice down to cutting board. Repeat slicing all the way around onion to make 12 to 16 evenly spaced cuts. Turn onion over; gently separate outer pieces.

3. Meanwhile, put flour in large bowl. Whisk buttermilk and eggs in another large bowl. Combine panko, paprika and seafood seasoning in another bowl.

4. Coat onion with flour, shaking off any excess. Dip onion in egg mixture, letting excess drip back into bowl. Then coat evenly with panko.

5. Preheat air fryer to 390°F. Spray basket with nonstick cooking spray.

6. Cook 10 to 12 minutes or until golden brown and crispy. Serve immediately with dipping sauce.

Calories 170, **Total Fat** 8g, **Saturated Fat** 1.5g, **Cholesterol** 70mg, **Sodium** 420mg, **Carbohydrates** 19g, **Dietary Fiber** 1g, **Protein** 4g

CAPRESE-STYLE TARTLETS

MAKES 6 TARTLETS

3 tomatoes, cut into
   4 slices each

3 tablespoons
   prepared pesto
   sauce

1 sheet frozen puff
   pastry (half
   of 17¼-ounce
   package)

6 ounces fresh
   mozzarella cheese

2 tablespoons chopped
   kalamata olives

1. Place tomatoes in large resealable food storage bag. Add pesto; toss to coat. Marinate at room temperature 30 minutes.

2. Unfold puff pastry; thaw 20 minutes on lightly floured surface.

3. Preheat air fryer to 370°F. Line basket with parchment paper.

4. Cut out six 4-inch rounds from pastry. Top each round with two tomato slices. Cook in batches 8 to 10 minutes or until pastry is light golden and puffed.

5. Cut mozzarella into six ¼-inch-thick slices. Top each tart with one mozzarella slice. Cook in batches 1 minute or until cheese is melted. Top tarts evenly with olives. Serve warm.

Calories 160, **Total Fat** 11g, **Saturated Fat** 5g, **Cholesterol** 20mg, **Sodium** 250mg, **Carbohydrates** 6g, **Dietary Fiber** 1g, **Protein** 7g

BUFFALO CAULIFLOWER BITES

MAKES 4 SERVINGS

½ cup all-purpose flour

½ cup water

½ teaspoon garlic powder

½ teaspoon salt

¼ teaspoon black pepper

1 small head cauliflower, cut into small florets

3 tablespoons hot pepper sauce

1 tablespoon melted butter

Chopped fresh parsley

Blue cheese dressing and celery sticks

1. Preheat air fryer to 390°F. Line basket with parchment paper.

2. Combine flour, water, garlic powder, salt and pepper in large bowl; stir until mixed. Add cauliflower; stir until florets are well coated.

3. Cook 8 to 10 minutes, shaking occasionally during cooking, until florets are slightly tender and browned.

4. Meanwhile, combine hot pepper sauce and butter in medium bowl. Add warm florets; toss well.

5. Sprinkle with parsley. Serve with blue cheese dressing and celery sticks.

Calories 80, **Total Fat** 5g, **Saturated Fat** 0g, **Cholesterol** 0mg, **Sodium** 820mg, **Carbohydrates** 16g, **Dietary Fiber** 2g, **Protein** 3g

SPINACH CHEESE BUNDLES

MAKES 32 BUNDLES (8 SERVINGS)

1 package (17¼ ounces) frozen puff pastry (2 sheets)

1 package (6½ ounces) garlic-and-herb spreadable cheese

½ cup packed chopped spinach

¼ teaspoon black pepper

Sweet and sour sauce (optional)

1. Unfold puff pasty; thaw 20 minutes on lightly floured surface. Cut each 12-inch square into 16 (3-inch) squares.

2. Preheat air fryer to 370°F.

3. Combine cheese, spinach and pepper in small bowl; mix well.

4. Place about 1 teaspoon cheese mixture in center of each pastry square. Brush edges of squares with water. Bring edges together over filling; twist tightly to seal. Fan out corners of puff pastry.

5. Cook in batches 8 to 10 minutes or until golden brown. Serve warm with sweet and sour sauce, if desired.

Calories 80, **Total Fat** 5g, **Saturated Fat** 2g, **Cholesterol** 10mg, **Sodium** 340mg, **Carbohydrates** 5g, **Dietary Fiber** 0g, **Protein** 4g

FRIED PICKLE SPEARS

MAKES 6 SERVINGS

2 tablespoons
  all-purpose flour

½ teaspoon cornstarch

2 eggs

½ cup cornflake crumbs

6 pickle spears, patted
  dry

  Yellow mustard,
    spicy grain mustard
    or honey mustard
    (optional)

1. Combine flour and cornstarch in small bowl. Beat eggs in another small bowl; set aside. Place cornflake crumbs in shallow plate.

2. Coat pickle spears in flour mixture, shaking off excess flour. Dip pickles in eggs; roll in cornflake crumbs.

3. Preheat air fryer to 390°F. Line basket with foil or parchment paper. Cook in batches 10 to 12 minutes or until golden brown. Remove to serving dish. Serve with mustard, if desired.

Calories 70, **Total Fat** 1.5g, **Saturated Fat** 0.5g, **Cholesterol** 60mg, **Sodium** 360mg, **Carbohydrates** 10g, **Dietary Fiber** 0g, **Protein** 3g

MINI CHICKPEA CAKES

MAKES 2 DOZEN CAKES (8 SERVINGS)

1 can (about 15 ounces) chickpeas, rinsed and drained

1 cup grated carrots

⅓ cup seasoned dry bread crumbs

¼ cup creamy Italian salad dressing, plus additional for dipping

1 egg

1. Preheat air fryer to 370°F. Spray basket with nonstick cooking spray.

2. Coarsely mash chickpeas in medium bowl with a fork or potato masher. Stir in carrots, bread crumbs, ¼ cup salad dressing and egg; mix well.

3. Shape chickpea mixture into 24 patties, using about 1 tablespoon mixture for each.

4. Cook in batches 10 minutes, turning halfway through cooking, until lightly browned. Serve warm with additional salad dressing for dipping, if desired.

Calories 120, **Total Fat** 6g, **Saturated Fat** 1g, **Cholesterol** 25mg, **Sodium** 240mg, **Carbohydrates** 12g, **Dietary Fiber** 2g, **Protein** 4g

CRISPY MUSTARD CHICKEN
(page 74)

CHAPTER 3

SUPER SUPPERS

BEER AIR-FRIED CHICKEN

MAKES 4 SERVINGS

1⅓ cups light-colored beer, such as pale ale

2 tablespoons buttermilk

1¼ cups panko bread crumbs

½ cup grated Parmesan cheese

4 chicken breast cutlets (about 1¼ pounds)

½ teaspoon salt

¼ teaspoon black pepper

1. Preheat air fryer to 370°F. Line basket with foil; spray with nonstick cooking spray.

2. Combine beer and buttermilk in shallow bowl. Combine panko and cheese in another shallow bowl.

3. Sprinkle chicken with salt and pepper. Dip in beer mixture; roll in panko mixture to coat.

4. Cook in batches 18 to 20 minutes or until chicken is no longer pink in center.

TIP: To make a substitution for buttermilk, place 1 teaspoon lemon juice or distilled whiwte vinegar in a measuring cup and add enough milk to measure ⅓ cup. Stir and let the mixture stand at room temperature for 5 minutes. Discard leftover mixture.

Calories 340, **Total Fat** 6g, **Saturated Fat** 3g, **Cholesterol** 85mg, **Sodium** 680mg, **Carbohydrates** 22g, **Dietary Fiber** 0g, **Protein** 42g

FRIED TOFU WITH SESAME DIPPING SAUCE

MAKES 4 SERVINGS

- 3 tablespoons soy sauce or tamari

- 2 tablespoons unseasoned rice vinegar

- 2 teaspoons sugar

- 1 teaspoon sesame seeds, toasted*

- 1 teaspoon dark sesame oil

- ⅛ teaspoon red pepper flakes

- 1 package (about 14 ounces) extra firm tofu

- ¼ cup all-purpose flour

- 1 egg

- 1 cup panko bread crumbs

  Salt

To toast sesame seeds, spread seeds in small skillet. Shake skillet over medium-low heat about 3 minutes or until seeds begin to pop and turn golden.

1. Whisk soy sauce, vinegar, sugar, sesame seeds, sesame oil and red pepper flakes in small bowl until well blended; set aside.

2. Drain tofu and press between paper towels to remove excess water. Cut crosswise into four slices; cut each slice diagonally into triangles. Place flour in shallow dish. Beat egg in shallow bowl. Place panko in another shallow bowl.

3. Dip each piece of tofu in flour, turning to lightly coat all sides. Dip in egg, letting excess drip back into bowl. Roll in panko to coat. Season with salt.

4. Preheat air fryer to 390°F. Spray tofu with nonstick cooking spray. Cook in batches 5 to 6 minutes or until golden brown. Serve with sauce for dipping.

Calories 250, **Total Fat** 9g, **Saturated Fat** 1g, **Cholesterol** 45mg, **Sodium** 930mg, **Carbohydrates** 25g, **Dietary Fiber** 0g, **Protein** 17g

BREADED VEAL SCALLOPINI WITH MUSHROOMS

MAKES 2 SERVINGS

½ pound veal cutlets

¼ teaspoon salt

⅛ teaspoon black pepper

1 egg

1 tablespoon water

½ cup plain dry bread crumbs

1 tablespoon unsalted butter

2 large shallots, chopped (about ¼ cup)

8 ounces exotic mushrooms, such as cremini, oyster, baby bella and shiitake*

½ teaspoon herbes de Provence**

½ cup reduced-sodium chicken broth

2 lemon wedges (optional)

Exotic mushrooms make this dish special. However, you can substitute white button mushrooms, if you prefer.

**Herbes de Provence is a mixture of basil, fennel, lavender, marjoram, rosemary, sage, savory and thyme used to season meat, poultry and vegetables.*

1. Season cutlets with salt and pepper. Lightly beat egg with water in shallow dish. Place bread crumbs in separate shallow dish.

2. Dip cutlet into egg, letting excess drip off. Dip in crumbs, turning to coat. Repeat with remaining cutlets.

3. Preheat air fryer to 370°F. Spray basket with nonstick cooking spray. Cook 12 to 15 minutes, turning halfway, until golden brown and cooked through. Transfer to plate.

4. Heat butter in large medium skillet over medium-high heat. Add shallots; cook and stir 1 to 2 minutes or until translucent. Add mushrooms and herbes de Provence; cook and stir 3 to 4 minutes or until most of liquid is evaporated. Stir in broth; cook 2 to 3 minutes or until slightly thickened.

5. Pour mushroom mixture over cutlets. Garnish with lemon wedges.

Calories 450, **Total Fat** 22g, **Saturated Fat** 10g, **Cholesterol** 195mg, **Sodium** 720mg, **Carbohydrates** 29g, **Dietary Fiber** 1g, **Protein** 33g

GARLICKY AIR-FRIED CHICKEN THIGHS

MAKES 4 SERVINGS

1 egg

2 tablespoons water

1 cup plain dry bread crumbs

1 teaspoon salt

1 teaspoon garlic powder

½ teaspoon black pepper

¼ teaspoon ground red pepper

8 chicken thighs (about 3 pounds)

1. Preheat air fryer to 390°F.

2. Beat egg and water in shallow bowl. Combine bread crumbs, salt, garlic powder, black pepper and ground red pepper in separate shallow bowl.

3. Dip chicken into egg mixture; turn to coat. Transfer to bread crumb mixture; press lightly to coat both sides.

4. Lightly spray chicken with nonstick cooking spray. Cook 20 to 22 minutes or until browned and cooked through.

VARIATIONS: Substitute seasoned bread crumbs for the plain bread crumbs, garlic powder, ground red pepper, salt and black pepper. Or, substitute your favorite dried herbs or spices for the garlic powder and ground red pepper; thyme, sage, oregano or rosemary would be delicious, as would Cajun or Creole seasoning.

Calories 380, **Total Fat** 11g, **Saturated Fat** 3g, **Cholesterol** 240mg, **Sodium** 700mg, **Carbohydrates** 20g, **Dietary Fiber** 0g, **Protein** 45g

SALMON CROQUETTES

MAKES 10 CROQUETTES (5 SERVINGS)

1 can (14¾ ounces) pink salmon, drained and flaked

½ cup mashed potatoes*

1 egg, beaten

3 tablespoons diced red bell pepper

2 tablespoons sliced green onion

1 tablespoon chopped fresh parsley

½ cup seasoned dry bread crumbs

Use mashed potatoes that are freshly made, leftover, or potatoes made from instant potatoes.

1. Combine salmon, potatoes, egg, bell pepper, green onion and parsley in medium bowl; mix well.

2. Place bread crumbs on medium plate. Shape salmon mixture into 10 croquettes about 3 inches long by 1 inch wide. Roll croquettes in crumbs to coat. Refrigerate 15 to 20 minutes or until firm.

3. Preheat air fryer to 350°F. Cook in batches 6 to 8 minutes or until browned. Serve immediately.

Calories 200, **Total Fat** 6g, **Saturated Fat** 1.5g, **Cholesterol** 110mg, **Sodium** 560mg, **Carbohydrates** 12g, **Dietary Fiber** 0g, **Protein** 24g

AIR-FRIED CAJUN BASS

MAKES 4 SERVINGS

2 tablespoons all-purpose flour

1 to 1½ teaspoons Cajun or Caribbean jerk seasoning

1 egg white

2 teaspoons water

⅓ cup seasoned dry bread crumbs

2 tablespoons cornmeal

4 skinless striped bass, halibut or cod fillets (4 to 6 ounces each), thawed if frozen

Chopped fresh parsley (optional)

4 lemon wedges

1. Combine flour and Cajun seasoning in medium resealable food storage bag. Whisk egg white and water in small bowl. Combine bread crumbs and cornmeal in separate small bowl.

2. Working one at a time, add fillet to bag; shake to coat evenly. Dip in egg white mixture, letting excess drip back into bowl. Roll in bread crumb mixture, pressing lightly to adhere. Repeat with remaining fillets.

3. Preheat air fryer to 390°F. Cook in batches 8 to 10 minutes, turning halfway through cooking, until golden brown, fish is opaque in center and flakes easily when tested with fork.

4. Sprinkle parsley over fish, if desired. Serve with lemon wedges.

Calories 200, **Total Fat** 5g, **Saturated Fat** 1g, **Cholesterol** 75mg, **Sodium** 260mg, **Carbohydrates** 14g, **Dietary Fiber** 0g, **Protein** 24g

CHICKEN WITH HERB STUFFING

MAKES 4 SERVINGS

⅓ cup fresh basil leaves

1 package (8 ounces) goat cheese with garlic and herbs

4 boneless skinless chicken breasts

1 tablespoon olive oil

1. Place basil in food processor; process using on/off pulsing action until chopped. Cut goat cheese into large pieces and add to food processor; process using on/off pulsing action until combined.

2. Preheat air fryer to 370°F. Place 1 chicken breast on cutting board and cover with plastic wrap. Pound with meat mallet until ¼ inch thick. Repeat with remaining chicken.

3. Shape about 2 tablespoons of cheese mixture into log and set in center of each chicken breast. Wrap chicken around filling to enclose completely. Tie securely with kitchen string. Drizzle with oil.

4. Cook 15 to 20 minutes or until chicken is cooked through and filling is hot. Allow to cool slightly, remove string and slice to serve.

Calories 330, **Total Fat** 21g, **Saturated Fat** 9g, **Cholesterol** 145mg, **Sodium** 280mg, **Carbohydrates** 2g, **Dietary Fiber** 0g, **Protein** 37g

VEGGIE PIZZA PITAS

MAKES 2 SERVINGS

1 whole wheat pita bread round, cut in half horizontally (to make 2 rounds)

2 tablespoons pizza sauce

½ teaspoon dried basil

⅛ teaspoon red pepper flakes (optional)

½ cup sliced mushrooms

¼ cup thinly sliced green bell pepper

¼ cup thinly sliced red onion

½ cup (4 ounces) shredded mozzarella cheese

1 teaspoon grated Parmesan cheese

1. Preheat air fryer to 370°F.

2. Arrange pita rounds, rough sides up, in single layer on parchment paper. Spread 1 tablespoon pizza sauce evenly over each round to within ¼ inch of edge. Sprinkle with basil and red pepper flakes, if desired. Top with mushrooms, bell pepper and onion. Sprinkle with mozzarella cheese.

3. Cook 5 to 7 minutes until mozzarella cheese melts. Sprinkle ½ teaspoon Parmesan cheese over each round.

Calories 113, **Total Fat** 2g, **Saturated Fat** 1g, **Cholesterol** 6mg, **Sodium** 402mg, **Carbohydrates** 13g, **Dietary Fiber** 2g, **Protein** 11g

FRIED CHICKEN FINGERS WITH DIPPING SAUCE

MAKES 4 SERVINGS

¼ cup plain yogurt

2 tablespoons honey

2 tablespoons prepared mustard

2 teaspoons cider vinegar

1 tablespoon sugar

¼ teaspoon ground cinnamon

1 teaspoon paprika

½ teaspoon garlic powder

½ teaspoon salt, divided

¼ teaspoon black pepper

1½ cups panko bread crumbs

⅓ cup buttermilk

2 egg whites

8 chicken tenders (about 1¼ pounds)

1. For dipping sauce, combine yogurt, honey, mustard, vinegar, sugar and cinnamon in small bowl; set aside.

2. Combine paprika, garlic powder, ¼ teaspoon salt and black pepper in small bowl; set aside. Place panko in shallow dish. Whisk buttermilk and egg whites in medium bowl. Add chicken to buttermilk mixture; toss until well coated.

3. Coat chicken with panko, one piece at a time, pressing down lightly to adhere. Sprinkle chicken evenly with paprika mixture.

4. Preheat air fryer to 390°F. Line basket with parchment paper.

5. Cook in batches 10 to 12 minutes or until chicken is golden brown and crispy and no longer pink in center.

6. Sprinkle chicken with remaining ¼ teaspoon salt, if desired. Serve with sauce.

Calories 335, **Total Fat** 10g, **Saturated Fat** 1g, **Cholesterol** 83mg, **Sodium** 554mg, **Carbohydrates** 22g, **Dietary Fiber** 1g, **Protein** 39g

BREADED PORK CUTLETS WITH TONKATSU SAUCE

MAKES 4 SERVINGS

Tonkatsu Sauce
(recipe follows)

½ cup all-purpose flour

2 eggs, beaten with
2 tablespoons water

1½ cups panko bread crumbs

1 pound pork tenderloin,
trimmed of fat and sliced
into ½-inch-thick pieces

2 cups hot cooked rice

1. Prepare Tonkatsu Sauce; set aside. Preheat air fryer to 370°F.

2. Place flour in shallow plate. Place eggs in shallow bowl. Spread panko on medium plate. Dip each pork slice first in flour, then egg. Shake off excess and coat in panko.

3. Cook 12 to 15 minutes or until cooked through.

4. Serve over rice with Tonkatsu Sauce.

TONKATSU SAUCE

MAKES ABOUT ⅓ CUP SAUCE

¼ cup ketchup

1 tablespoon soy sauce

2 teaspoons sugar

2 teaspoons mirin (Japanese
sweet rice wine)

1 teaspoon Worcestershire sauce

½ teaspoon grated fresh ginger

1 clove garlic, minced

Combine ketchup, soy sauce, sugar, mirin, Worcestershire sauce, ginger and garlic in small bowl.

Calories 460, **Total Fat** 5g, **Saturated Fat** 1.5g, **Cholesterol** 160mg, **Sodium** 630mg, **Carbohydrates** 64g, **Dietary Fiber** 0g, **Protein** 34g

ROASTED ALMOND TILAPIA

MAKES 2 SERVINGS

2 tilapia or Boston scrod fillets (6 ounces each)

¼ teaspoon salt

1 tablespoon prepared mustard

¼ cup all-purpose flour

2 tablespoons chopped almonds

Paprika (optional)

Lemon wedges (optional)

1. Preheat air fryer to 370°F. Line basket with parchment paper.

2. Season fish with salt. Spread mustard over fish. Combine flour and almonds in small bowl; sprinkle over fish. Press lightly to adhere. Sprinkle with paprika, if desired.

3. Cook in batches 12 to 15 minutes or until fish is opaque in center and begins to flake when tested with fork. Serve with lemon wedges, if desired.

Calories 272, **Total Fat** 6g, **Saturated Fat** 2g, **Cholesterol** 84mg, **Sodium** 464mg, **Carbohydrates** 17g, **Dietary Fiber** 1g, **Protein** 37g

BAKED PANKO CHICKEN

MAKES 2 SERVINGS

½ cup panko bread crumbs

3 teaspoons assorted dried herbs (such as rosemary, basil, parsley, thyme or oregano), divided

Salt and black pepper

2 tablespoons mayonnaise

2 boneless skinless chicken breasts

1. Preheat air fryer to 390°F. Line basket with parchment paper; spray with nonstick cooking spray.

2. Combine panko, 1 teaspoon herbs, salt and pepper on shallow plate. Combine mayonnaise and remaining 2 teaspoons herbs in small bowl. Spread mayonnaise mixture onto chicken. Coat chicken with panko mixture, pressing to adhere.

3. Cook 18 to 20 until chicken is browned and no longer pink in center.

Calories 280, **Total Fat** 12g, **Saturated Fat** 1.5g, **Cholesterol** 70mg, **Sodium** 190mg, **Carbohydrates** 15g, **Dietary Fiber** 0g, **Protein** 28g

DILLED SALMON IN PARCHMENT

MAKES 2 SERVINGS

2 skinless salmon fillets
  (4 ounces each)

1 tablespoon butter,
  melted

1 tablespoon lemon
  juice

1 tablespoon chopped
  fresh dill

1 tablespoon chopped
  shallots

¼ teaspoon salt

⅛ teaspoon black
  pepper

1. Preheat air fryer to 370°F. Cut two pieces of parchment paper into 12-inch squares. Place fish fillet on parchment.

2. Combine butter and lemon juice in small bowl; drizzle over fish. Sprinkle with dill, shallots and salt and pepper. Wrap parchment around fish.

3. Cook 6 to 8 minutes or until fish is cooked through and easily flakes when tested with a fork.

Calories 290, **Total Fat** 21g, **Saturated Fat** 7g, **Cholesterol** 80mg, **Sodium** 360mg, **Carbohydrates** 1g, **Dietary Fiber** 0g, **Protein** 23g

FRIED TOFU WITH ASIAN VEGETABLES

MAKES 6 SERVINGS

1 pound firm tofu

¼ cup soy sauce, divided

1 cup all-purpose flour

⅛ teaspoon black pepper

1 package (16 ounces) frozen mixed Asian vegetables*

3 tablespoons water

1 teaspoon cornstarch

3 tablespoons plum sauce

2 tablespoons lemon juice

2 teaspoons sugar

1 teaspoon minced fresh ginger

⅛ to ¼ teaspoon red pepper flakes

Frozen vegetables do not need to be thawed before cooking.

1. Drain tofu; cut into ¾-inch cubes. Gently mix tofu and 2 tablespoons soy sauce in shallow bowl; let stand 5 minutes. Combine flour and black pepper on plate. Gently toss tofu cubes, a small amount at a time, with flour mixture to coat. Spray tofu with nonstick cooking spray.

2. Preheat air fryer to 390°F. Cook in batches 3 to 4 minutes or until browned. Remove to plate; keep warm.

3. Place frozen vegetables in basket. Cook 3 to 4 minutes, shaking halfway through cooking, until vegetables are heated through. Set aside; cover to keep warm.

4. Stir water into cornstarch in small bowl until well blended. Combine cornstarch mixture, remaining 2 tablespoons soy sauce, plum sauce, lemon juice, sugar, ginger and red pepper flakes in medium microwavable bowl; cover and heat in microwave on HIGH 1 minute or until sauce is slightly thickened; stir to mix well. Spoon vegetables into serving bowl. Top with tofu and sauce; toss gently to mix.

Calories 190, **Total Fat** 4.5g, **Saturated Fat** 0g, **Cholesterol** 0mg, **Sodium** 860mg, **Carbohydrates** 25g, **Dietary Fiber** 0g, **Protein** 12g

CRISPY MUSTARD CHICKEN

MAKES 4 SERVINGS

4 bone-in chicken breasts

½ teaspoon salt

¼ teaspoon black pepper

⅓ cup Dijon mustard

½ cup panko bread crumbs or plain dry bread crumbs

1. Preheat air fryer to 370°F. Line basket with foil; spray with nonstick cooking spray.

2. Season chicken with salt and pepper. Cook 20 minutes.

3. Brush chicken generously with mustard. Sprinkle with panko, gently pressing panko into mustard. Cook 6 to 8 minutes or until chicken is golden brown and cooked through.

Calories 200, **Total Fat** 3g, **Saturated Fat** 0.5g, **Cholesterol** 85mg, **Sodium** 800mg, **Carbohydrates** 8g, **Dietary Fiber** 0g, **Protein** 28g

SALMON-POTATO CAKES WITH MUSTARD TARTAR SAUCE

MAKES 2 SERVINGS

3 small unpeeled red potatoes (8 ounces), halved

1 cup water

1 cup flaked cooked salmon

2 green onions, chopped

1 egg white

2 tablespoons chopped fresh parsley, divided

½ teaspoon Cajun or Creole seasoning

1 tablespoon mayonnaise

1 tablespoon plain fat-free yogurt or fat-free sour cream

2 teaspoons coarse grain mustard

1 tablespoon chopped dill pickle

1 teaspoon lemon juice

1. Place potatoes and water in medium saucepan. Bring to a boil. Reduce heat and simmer about 15 minutes or until potatoes are tender. Drain. Mash potatoes with fork, leaving chunky texture.

2. Combine mashed potatoes, salmon, green onions, egg white, 1 tablespoon parsley and Cajun seasoning in medium bowl.

3. Preheat air fryer to 370°F. Gently shape salmon mixture into two patties; flatten slightly. Cook 5 to 6 minutes, turning halfway through cooking, until browned and heated through.

4. Meanwhile, combine mayonnaise, yogurt, mustard, remaining 1 tablespoon parsley, pickle and lemon juice in small bowl. Serve sauce with cakes.

Calories 276, **Total Fat** 11g, **Saturated Fat** 2g, **Cholesterol** 52mg, **Sodium** 300mg, **Carbohydrates** 24g, **Dietary Fiber** 2g, **Protein** 19g

CHICKEN PISTACHIO

MAKES 4 SERVINGS

4 boneless skinless chicken breasts

4 sheets (18×12 inches each) heavy duty foil, lightly sprayed with nonstick cooking spray

1 tablespoon olive oil

¼ teaspoon paprika

¼ cup finely chopped pistachio nuts

2 tablespoons finely chopped green onion

Lemon slices (optional)

1. Preheat air fryer to 370°F. Place chicken breasts on foil sheets. Brush chicken with oil; sprinkle with paprika. Double fold sides and ends of foil to seal packets, leaving head space for heat circulation. Place packets in air fryer basket.

2. Cook 25 minutes. Remove from air fryer. Carefully open one end of foil packet to allow steam to escape. Open foil completely; sprinkle chicken with pistachios and green onion. Leave foil open and return to air fryer. Cook about 5 minutes or until chicken is no longer pink in center (165°F).

3. Transfer contents of packets to serving plates. Garnish with lemon slices.

Calories 220, **Total Fat** 10g, **Saturated Fat** 1.5g, **Cholesterol** 85mg, **Sodium** 55mg, **Carbohydrates** 2g, **Dietary Fiber** 1g, **Protein** 28g

TERIYAKI SALMON

MAKES 2 SERVINGS

¼ cup dark sesame oil

Juice of 1 lemon

¼ cup soy sauce

2 tablespoons packed brown sugar

1 clove garlic, minced

2 salmon fillets (about 4 ounces each)

Hot cooked rice

Toasted sesame seeds and green onions (optional)

1. Whisk oil, lemon juice, soy sauce, brown sugar and garlic in medium bowl. Place salmon in large resealable food storage bag; add marinade. Refrigerate at least 2 hours.

2. Preheat air fryer to 350°F. Spray basket with nonstick cooking spray.

3. Cook 8 to 10 minutes until salmon is crispy and easily flakes with a fork. Serve with rice and garnish as desired.

Calories 320, **Total Fat** 22g, **Saturated Fat** 4.5g, **Cholesterol** 60mg, **Sodium** 650mg, **Carbohydrates** 4g, **Dietary Fiber** 0g, **Protein** 24g

CHICKEN SALAD WITH CREAMY TARRAGON DRESSING

MAKES 4 SERVINGS

Creamy Tarragon Dressing (recipe follows)

1 pound chicken tenders

1 teaspoon Cajun or Creole seasoning*

1 package (10 ounces) mixed salad greens

2 unpeeled apples, cored and thinly sliced

1 cup packed alfalfa sprouts

2 tablespoons raisins

Adjust your seasoning if you prefer more or less of a spicier taste.

1. Prepare Creamy Tarragon Dressing. Preheat air fryer to 370°F.

2. Season chicken with Cajun seasoning. Spray chicken with nonstick cooking spray. Cook in batches 10 to 12 minutes or until no longer pink in center.

3. Divide salad greens among four large plates. Arrange chicken, apples and sprouts on top of greens. Sprinkle with raisins. Serve with dressing.

CREAMY TARRAGON DRESSING

MAKES ABOUT 1 CUP

½ cup plain yogurt

¼ cup sour cream

¼ cup frozen apple juice concentrate

1 tablespoon spicy brown mustard

1 tablespoon minced fresh tarragon leaves

Combine all ingredients in small bowl.

Calories 276, **Total Fat** 5g, **Saturated Fat** 1g, **Cholesterol** 74mg, **Sodium** 204mg, **Carbohydrates** 29g, **Dietary Fiber** 3g, **Protein** 30g

RICOTTA AND SPINACH HASSELBACK CHICKEN

MAKES 2 SERVINGS

½ cup fresh baby spinach leaves

1 teaspoon olive oil

2 tablespoons reduced-fat ricotta cheese

2 boneless skinless chicken breasts (about 6 ounces each)

¼ teaspoon salt

⅛ teaspoon black pepper

2 tablespoons shredded Cheddar cheese

1. Preheat air fryer to 390°F. Line basket with foil.

2. Place spinach and oil in small microwavable dish. Microwave on HIGH 20 to 30 seconds or until spinach is slightly wilted. Stir ricotta cheese into spinach; mix well.

3. Cut four diagonal slits three fourths of the way into each chicken breast (do not cut all the way through). Place about 1 teaspoon ricotta mixture into each slit. Sprinkle chicken with salt and pepper.

4. Cook 12 minutes. Top chicken with Cheddar cheese.

5. Cook 4 to 6 minutes or until cheese melts, chicken is golden and juices run clear.

Calories 250, **Total Fat** 9g, **Saturated Fat** 4g, **Cholesterol** 95mg, **Sodium** 790mg, **Carbohydrates** 2g, **Dietary Fiber** 0g, **Protein** 36g

SPICY SALMON

MAKES 4 SERVINGS

½ teaspoon ground cumin

½ teaspoon chili powder

½ teaspoon salt

¼ teaspoon black pepper

¼ teaspoon paprika

4 salmon fillets (about 4 ounces each)

1. Preheat air fryer to 330°F. Line basket with parchment paper; spray with nonstick cooking spray.

2. Combine cumin, chili powder, salt, pepper and paprika in small bowl. Rub over top of salmon.

3. Cook 8 to 10 minutes or until salmon is lightly crispy and easily flakes with a fork.

SERVING SUGGESTION: Serve with tossed salad and rice.

Calories 149, **Total Fat** 5g, **Saturated Fat** 1g, **Cholesterol** 53mg, **Sodium** 235mg, **Carbohydrates** 0g, **Dietary Fiber** 0g, **Protein** 24g

JAPANESE FRIED CHICKEN ON WATERCRESS

MAKES 4 SERVINGS

1 pound boneless skinless chicken breasts, cut into 2-inch pieces

3 tablespoons tamari or soy sauce

2 tablespoons sake

3 cloves garlic, minced

1 teaspoon minced fresh ginger

⅓ cup cornstarch

3 tablespoons all-purpose flour

Salad

¼ cup unseasoned rice vinegar

3 teaspoons tamari or soy sauce

1 teaspoon dark sesame oil

2 bunches watercress, trimmed of tough stems

1 pint grape tomatoes, halved

1. Place chicken in large resealable food storage bag. Mix 3 tablespoons tamari, sake, garlic and ginger in small bowl. Pour over chicken and marinate in refrigerator at least 30 minutes, turning bag occasionally.

2. Meanwhile, preheat air fryer to 390°F. Combine cornstarch and flour in shallow dish. Drain chicken and discard marinade. Roll chicken pieces in cornstarch mixture and shake off excess.

3. Cook in batches 8 to 10 minutes or until chicken is golden brown.

4. For salad, whisk together vinegar, 3 teaspoons tamari and sesame oil in small bowl. Arrange watercress and tomatoes on serving plates. Drizzle with dressing and top with chicken.

Calories 210, **Total Fat** 3g, **Saturated Fat** 0.5g, **Cholesterol** 55mg, **Sodium** 1250mg, **Carbohydrates** 24g, **Dietary Fiber** 1g, **Protein** 27g

BLACKENED CATFISH WITH EASY TARTAR SAUCE AND RICE

MAKES 4 SERVINGS

Easy Tartar Sauce
(recipe follows)

4 catfish fillets (4 ounces each)

2 teaspoons lemon juice

2 teaspoons blackened or Cajun seasoning

1 cup hot cooked rice (optional)

1. Prepare Easy Tartar Sauce.

2. Rinse catfish and pat dry with paper towel. Sprinkle with lemon juice; coat with nonstick cooking spray. Sprinkle with seasoning blend; coat again with cooking spray.

3. Preheat air fryer to 390°F. Cook in batches 8 to 10 minutes, turning halfway through cooking, until fish begins to easily flake when tested with a fork. Serve with Easy Tartar Sauce and rice, if desired.

EASY TARTAR SAUCE

MAKES ABOUT ¼ CUP SAUCE

¼ cup mayonnaise

2 tablespoons sweet pickle relish

1 teaspoon lemon juice

Combine mayonnaise, relish and lemon juice in small bowl; mix well. Cover and refrigerate until ready to serve.

Calories 290, **Total Fat** 8g, **Saturated Fat** 2g, **Cholesterol** 54mg, **Sodium** 344mg, **Carbohydrates** 33g, **Dietary Fiber** 1g, **Protein** 19g

CHICKEN WITH KALE STUFFING

MAKES 4 SERVINGS

4 boneless skinless chicken breasts

1 cup sliced mushrooms

½ cup chopped onion

2 tablespoons dry white wine

1 teaspoon chopped fresh oregano *or* ¼ teaspoon dried oregano

1 clove garlic, minced

½ teaspoon black pepper

2 cups packed chopped stemmed kale

2 tablespoons light mayonnaise

½ cup seasoned dry bread crumbs

1. Preheat air fryer to 370°F. Spray basket with nonstick cooking spray; set aside. Trim fat from chicken. Pound chicken with meat mallet to ½-inch thickness; set aside.

2. Heat skillet over medium-high heat. Add mushrooms, onion, wine, oregano, garlic and pepper; cook and stir about 5 minutes or until onion is tender. Add kale; cook and stir until wilted.

3. Spread kale mixture evenly over flattened chicken breasts. Roll up chicken; secure with toothpicks. Brush chicken with mayonnaise; coat with bread crumbs.

4. Cook 15 to 20 minutes or until chicken is golden brown and no longer pink in center. Remove toothpicks before serving.

Calories 244, **Total Fat** 6g, **Saturated Fat** 1g, **Cholesterol** 76mg, **Sodium** 175mg, **Carbohydrates** 15g, **Dietary Fiber** 3g, **Protein** 30g

BUFFALO CHICKEN WRAPS
(page 98)

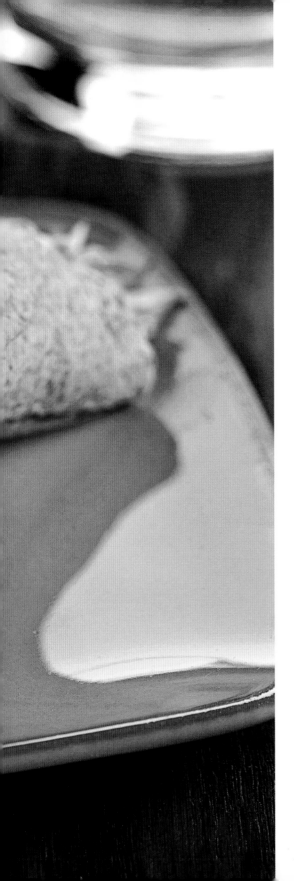

CHAPTER 4

SATISFYING SANDWICHES

SPICY EGGPLANT BURGERS

MAKES 4 SERVINGS

1 eggplant (about 1¼ pounds)

2 egg whites

½ cup Italian-style panko bread crumbs

3 tablespoons chipotle mayonnaise or regular mayonnaise

4 whole wheat hamburger buns, warmed

1½ cups loosely packed baby spinach

8 thin slices tomato

4 slices pepper jack cheese

1. Preheat air fryer to 370°F. Line basket with foil. Cut four ½-inch-thick slices from widest part of eggplant. Beat egg whites in shallow bowl. Place panko on medium plate.

2. Dip eggplant slices in egg whites; dredge in panko, pressing gently to adhere. Spray with nonstick cooking spray.

3. Cook in batches 6 to 8 minutes on each side or until golden brown.

4. Spread mayonnaise on bottom halves of buns; top with spinach, tomatoes, eggplant, cheese and tops of buns.

Calories 349, **Total Fat** 12g, **Saturated Fat** 3g, **Cholesterol** 20mg, **Sodium** 628mg, **Carbohydrates** 47g, **Dietary Fiber** 13g, **Protein** 16g

BUFFALO CHICKEN WRAPS

MAKES 2 SERVINGS

2 boneless skinless chicken breasts (about 4 ounces each)

4 tablespoons buffalo wing sauce, divided

1 cup broccoli slaw

1½ teaspoons light blue cheese salad dressing

2 (8-inch) whole wheat tortillas, warmed

1. Place chicken in large resealable food storage bag. Add 2 tablespoons buffalo sauce; seal bag. Marinate in refrigerator 15 minutes.

2. Meanwhile, preheat air fryer to 390°F. Cook 8 to 10 minutes per side or until no longer pink. When cool enough to handle, slice chicken; combine with remaining 2 tablespoons buffalo sauce in medium bowl.

3. Combine broccoli slaw and blue cheese dressing in medium bowl; mix well.

4. Arrange chicken and broccoli slaw evenly down center of each tortilla. Roll up to secure filling. To serve, cut in half diagonally.

TIP: If you don't like the spicy flavor of buffalo wing sauce, substitute your favorite barbecue sauce.

Calories 290, **Total Fat** 8g, **Saturated Fat** 2g, **Cholesterol** 65mg, **Sodium** 790mg, **Carbohydrates** 25g, **Dietary Fiber** 5g, **Protein** 28g

TUNA MELTS

MAKES 2 SERVINGS

1 can (about 5 ounces) chunk white tuna packed in water, drained and flaked

½ cup packaged coleslaw mix

1 tablespoon sliced green onion

1 tablespoon mayonnaise

½ tablespoon Dijon mustard

¼ teaspoon dried dill weed (optional)

2 English muffins, split

¼ cup (1 ounce) shredded Cheddar cheese

1. Preheat air fryer to 370°F. Combine tuna, coleslaw mix and green onion in medium bowl. Combine mayonnaise, mustard and dill weed, if desired, in small bowl. Stir mayonnaise mixture into tuna mixture. Spread tuna mixture onto muffin halves.

2. Cook 3 to 4 minutes or until heated through and lightly browned. Sprinkle with cheese. Cook 1 to 2 minutes until cheese melts.

Calories 294, **Total Fat** 6g, **Saturated Fat** 1g, **Cholesterol** 31mg, **Sodium** 459mg, **Carbohydrates** 29g, **Dietary Fiber** 2g, **Protein** 29g

MOZZARELLA & ROASTED RED PEPPER SANDWICH

MAKES 1 SANDWICH

1 tablespoon olive oil vinaigrette or Italian salad dressing

2 slices Italian-style sandwich bread (2 ounces)

2 fresh basil leaves

⅓ cup roasted red peppers, rinsed, drained and patted dry

1 to 2 slices (1 ounce each) part-skim mozzarella or Swiss cheese

1. Brush dressing on 1 side of 1 bread slice; top with basil, roasted peppers, cheese and remaining bread slice. Lightly spray both sides of sandwich with nonstick cooking spray.

2. Preheat air fryer to 350°F. Cook 4 to 5 minutes, turning halfway through cooking, until cheese melts and bread is golden brown.

Calories 303, **Total Fat** 9g, **Saturated Fat** 5g, **Cholesterol** 25mg, **Sodium** 727mg, **Carbohydrates** 35g, **Dietary Fiber** 2g, **Protein** 16g

PORTOBELLO MUSHROOM SANDWICH

MAKES 1 SERVING

1 large portobello
mushroom, cleaned
and stemmed

¼ medium green bell
pepper, halved

1 thin slice red onion

1 whole wheat
hamburger bun,
split and lightly
toasted

1 tablespoon fat-free
Italian salad
dressing

1 slice (1 ounce)
reduced-fat part-skim
mozzarella cheese
(optional)

1. Preheat air fryer to 390°F.

2. Brush mushroom, bell pepper, onion and cut
sides of bun with dressing; set bun aside.

3. Cook vegetables 6 to 8 minutes or until
vegetables are tender.

4. Top warm mushroom with cheese, if desired.
Cook 1 minute or until cheese is melted.

5. Cut pepper into strips. Place mushroom on
bottom half of bun; top with onion slice and
pepper strips. Cover with top half of bun.

Calories 160, **Total Fat** 2.5g, **Saturated Fat** 0g, **Cholesterol** 0mg,
Sodium 400mg, **Carbohydrates** 31g, **Dietary Fiber** 2g, **Protein** 6g

LENTIL BURGERS

MAKES 4 SERVINGS

1 can (about 14 ounces) vegetable broth

1 cup dried lentils, rinsed and sorted

1 small carrot, grated

¼ cup coarsely chopped mushrooms

1 egg

¼ cup plain dry bread crumbs

3 tablespoons finely chopped onion

2 to 4 cloves garlic, minced

1 teaspoon dried thyme

¼ cup plain fat-free yogurt

¼ cup chopped seeded cucumber

½ teaspoon dried mint

¼ teaspoon dried dill weed

¼ teaspoon black pepper

⅛ teaspoon salt

   Dash hot pepper sauce (optional)

   Kaiser rolls (optional)

1. Bring broth to a boil in medium saucepan over high heat. Stir in lentils; reduce heat to low. Simmer, covered, about 30 minutes or until lentils are tender and liquid is absorbed. Cool to room temperature.

2. Place lentils, carrot and mushrooms in food processor or blender; process until finely chopped but not smooth. (Some whole lentils should still be visible.) Stir in egg, bread crumbs, onion, garlic and thyme. Refrigerate, covered, 2 to 3 hours.

3. Shape lentil mixture into four (½-inch-thick) patties.

4. Preheat air fryer to 390°F. Spray basket with nonstick cooking spray. Cook patties in batches 8 to 10 minutes or until browned.

5. Meanwhile, for sauce, combine yogurt, cucumber, mint, dill weed, black pepper, salt and hot pepper sauce, if desired, in small bowl. Serve burgers on rolls with sauce.

Calories 124, **Total Fat** 2g, **Saturated Fat** 1g, **Cholesterol** 54mg, **Sodium** 166mg, **Carbohydrates** 21g, **Dietary Fiber** 1g, **Protein** 9g

FRIED CAULIFLOWER FLORETS
(page 126)

CHAPTER 5

SENSATIONAL SIDES

SWEET POTATO FRIES

MAKES 2 SERVINGS

2 sweet potatoes, peeled and sliced

1 tablespoon olive oil

¼ teaspoon coarse salt

¼ teaspoon black pepper

½ cup grated Parmesan cheese (optional)

1. Preheat air fryer to 390°F. Spray basket with nonstick cooking spray.

2. Toss potatoes with oil, salt and pepper in medium bowl.

3. Cook 10 to 12 minutes, shaking occasionally during cooking, until lightly browned. Sprinkle with cheese, if desired.

Calories 139, **Total Fat** 5g, **Saturated Fat** 1g, **Cholesterol** 0mg, **Sodium** 301mg, **Carbohydrates** 23g, **Dietary Fiber** 4g, **Protein** 2g

MEDITERRANEAN ROASTED TOMATOES

MAKES 4 SERVINGS

2 medium beefsteak tomatoes, cut in half crosswise

4 fresh basil leaves

2 tablespoons finely chopped pitted kalamata olives

2 tablespoons shredded mozzarella cheese

2 tablespoons grated Parmesan cheese

1. Preheat air fryer to 350°F. Place tomato halves in basket. Top each half with 1 fresh basil leaf and one fourth of olives and cheeses.

2. Cook 3 to 5 minutes or until cheese melts and begins to brown. Cool slightly before serving.

Calories 34, **Total Fat** 2g, **Saturated Fat** 1g, **Cholesterol** 4mg, **Sodium** 162mg, **Carbohydrates** 3g, **Dietary Fiber** 1g, **Protein** 2g

HASSELBACK POTATOES

MAKES 4 SERVINGS

4 small Yukon Gold
   potatoes

3 tablespoons butter,
   melted and divided

½ teaspoon salt

¼ teaspoon ground
   black pepper

¼ cup grated
   Parmesan cheese

   Chopped fresh
   parsley

1. Preheat air fryer to 390°F.

2. Cut diagonal slits into each potato about
   ⅛ inch apart and ¾ inches down (do not cut
   all the way through). Brush 2 tablespoons
   butter over tops; sprinkle with salt and
   pepper.

3. Cook 20 to 22 minutes or until slightly
   softened and lightly browned.

4. Brush potatoes with remaining butter.
   Sprinkle with cheese. Cook 3 to 5 minutes.
   Sprinkle with parsley.

Calories 230, **Total Fat** 11g, **Saturated Fat** 7g, **Cholesterol** 25mg, **Sodium** 440mg, **Carbohydrates** 27g, **Dietary Fiber** 3g, **Protein** 6g

GREEN BEAN FRIES

MAKES 6 SERVINGS

Dipping Sauce

½ cup light mayonnaise

¼ cup light sour cream

¼ cup low-fat buttermilk

¼ cup minced peeled cucumber

1½ teaspoons lemon juice

1 clove garlic

1 teaspoon wasabi powder

1 teaspoon prepared horseradish

½ teaspoon dried dill weed

½ teaspoon dried parsley flakes

½ teaspoon salt

⅛ teaspoon ground red pepper

Green Bean Fries

8 ounces fresh green beans, trimmed

⅓ cup all-purpose flour

⅓ cup cornstarch

½ cup reduced-fat (2%) milk

1 egg

¾ cup plain dry bread crumbs

1 teaspoon salt

½ teaspoon onion powder

¼ teaspoon garlic powder

1. For dipping sauce, combine mayonnaise, sour cream, buttermilk, cucumber, lemon juice, garlic, wasabi powder, horseradish, dill weed, parsley flakes, salt and ground red pepper in blender; blend until smooth. Refrigerate until ready to use.

2. For green bean fries, bring large saucepan of salted water to a boil. Add green beans; cook 4 minutes or until crisp-tender. Drain and run under cold running water to stop cooking.

3. Combine flour and cornstarch in large bowl. Whisk milk and egg in another large bowl. Combine bread crumbs, salt, onion powder and garlic powder in shallow bowl. Place green beans in flour mixture; toss to coat. Working in batches, coat beans with egg mixture, letting excess drain back into bowl. Roll green beans in bread crumb mixture to coat.

4. Preheat air fryer to 390°F. Cook in batches 6 to 8 minutes, shaking occasionally during cooking, until golden brown. Serve warm with dipping sauce.

Calories 230, **Total Fat** 10g, **Saturated Fat** 2.5g, **Cholesterol** 45mg, **Sodium** 760mg, **Carbohydrates** 29g, **Dietary Fiber** 1g, **Protein** 6g

AIR-FRIED CORN-ON-THE-COB

MAKES 2 SERVINGS

2 teaspoons butter,
 melted

¼ teaspoon salt

½ teaspoon black
 pepper

½ teaspoon chopped
 fresh parsley

2 ears corn, husks and
 silks removed

 Foil

 Grated Parmesan
 cheese (optional)

1. Preheat air fryer to 390°F. Combine butter, salt, pepper and parsley in small bowl. Brush corn with butter mixture. Wrap each ear corn in foil.*

2. Cook 10 to 12 minutes, turning halfway through cooking. Sprinkle with cheese before serving, if desired.

If your air fryer basket is on the smaller side, you may need to break ears of corn in half to fit.

Calories 110, **Total Fat** 5g, **Saturated Fat** 2.5g, **Cholesterol** 10mg, **Sodium** 310mg, **Carbohydrates** 17g, **Dietary Fiber** 3g, **Protein** 3g

ORANGE GLAZED CARROTS

MAKES 6 SERVINGS

1 package (32 ounces) baby carrots

1 tablespoon packed light brown sugar

1 tablespoon orange juice

1 tablespoon melted butter

¼ teaspoon ground cinnamon

⅛ teaspoon ground nutmeg

Orange peel and chopped fresh parsley (optional)

1. Preheat air fryer to 390°F.

2. Place carrots in large bowl. Combine brown sugar, orange juice and butter in small bowl. Pour over carrots; toss well.

3. Cook 6 to 8 minutes, shaking occasionally during cooking, until carrots are tender and lightly browned. Remove to serving dish. Sprinkle with cinnamon and nutmeg. Garnish with orange peel and parsley, if desired.

Calories 80, **Total Fat** 2g, **Saturated Fat** 1g, **Cholesterol** 5mg, **Sodium** 120mg, **Carbohydrates** 15g, **Dietary Fiber** 4g, **Protein** 1g

BUTTERNUT SQUASH FRIES

MAKES 4 SERVINGS

½ teaspoon garlic powder

¼ teaspoon salt

¼ teaspoon ground red
   pepper

1 butternut squash (about
   2½ pounds), peeled,
   seeded and cut into
   2-inch-thin slices

2 teaspoons vegetable oil

1. Combine garlic powder, salt and ground red pepper in small bowl; set aside.

2. Place squash in large bowl. Drizzle with oil and sprinkle with seasoning mix; gently toss to coat.

3. Preheat air fryer to 390°F. Cook in batches 16 to 18 minutes, shaking halfway during cooking, until squash is tender and begins to brown.

Calories 150, **Total Fat** 2.5g, **Saturated Fat** 0g, **Cholesterol** 0mg, **Sodium** 160mg, **Carbohydrates** 33g, **Dietary Fiber** 6g, **Protein** 3g

FRIED CAULIFLOWER FLORETS

MAKES 4 SERVINGS

1 head cauliflower

1 tablespoon olive oil

½ teaspoon salt

¼ teaspoon ground
   black pepper

½ teaspoon chopped
   fresh parsley

3 tablespoons grated
   Parmesan cheese

2 tablespoons panko
   bread crumbs

1. Preheat air fryer to 390°F. Spray basket with nonstick cooking spray.

2. Cut cauliflower into florets. Place in large bowl. Drizzle with oil. Sprinkle with salt, pepper and parsley.

3. Cook in batches 6 to 8 minutes until golden brown and slightly tender, shaking halfway through cooking.

4. Combine cheese and panko in small bowl. Sprinkle over top of cauliflower. Cook 2 to 3 minutes or until browned.

Calories 100, **Total Fat** 5g, **Saturated Fat** 1.5g, **Cholesterol** 0mg, **Sodium** 430mg, **Carbohydrates** 9g, **Dietary Fiber** 3g, **Protein** 5g

GREEN ONION-HERB CRESCENT ROLLS

MAKES 8 SERVINGS

1 package (8 ounces) refrigerated crescent roll dough (8 rolls)

3 tablespoons minced green onions

½ teaspoon Italian seasoning

1. Preheat air fryer to 370°F. Separate dough into eight triangles. Sprinkle about 1 teaspoon green onion over each triangle. Roll up loosely from wide end of each triangle to opposite point. Sprinkle with seasoning.

2. Cook in batches 5 to 6 minutes or until golden brown.

VARIATION: Other herbs and spices such as chopped fresh parsley, black pepper and sesame seeds can be used in place of the Italian seasoning.

Calories 102, **Total Fat** 5g, **Saturated Fat** 1g, **Cholesterol** 0mg, **Sodium** 233mg, **Carbohydrates** 12g, **Dietary Fiber** 1g, **Protein** 2g

GRILLED EGGPLANT ROLL-UPS

MAKES 2 SERVINGS

4 tablespoons hummus

4 slices Grilled
   Eggplant
   (recipe follows)

¼ cup crumbled feta
   cheese

¼ cup chopped green
   onions

4 tomato slices

1. Prepare Grilled Eggplant. Spread 1 tablespoon hummus on each eggplant slice. Top with feta, green onions and tomato.

2. Roll up tightly. Serve immediately.

GRILLED EGGPLANT: Preheat air fryer to 350°F. Spray basket with nonstick cooking spray. Sprinkle four 1-inch-thick eggplant slices with ½ teaspoon salt; let stand 15 minutes. Brush eggplant with olive oil. Cook in batches 5 minutes; turn and brush with olive oil. Cook 5 minutes or until tender.

Calories 96, **Total Fat** 6g, **Saturated Fat** 4g, **Cholesterol** 25mg, **Sodium** 326mg, **Carbohydrates** 5g, **Dietary Fiber** 1g, **Protein** 5g

ROASTED POTATOES AND ONIONS WITH HERBS

MAKES 4 SERVINGS

2 pounds unpeeled red potatoes, cut into 1½-inch pieces

1 sweet onion, such as Vidalia or Walla Walla, coarsely chopped

2 tablespoons olive oil

2 cloves garlic, minced

½ teaspoon salt

¼ teaspoon black pepper

¼ cup packed chopped mixed fresh herbs, such as basil, chives, parsley, oregano, rosemary leaves, sage, tarragon and thyme

1. Preheat air fryer to 390°F. Line basket with foil. Place potatoes and onion in large bowl.

2. Combine oil, garlic, salt and pepper in small bowl. Drizzle over potatoes and onion; toss well to coat.

3. Cook 18 to 20 minutes, shaking occasionally during cooking, until potatoes are tender and browned. Remove to large bowl. Add herbs; toss well.

Calories 240, **Total Fat** 7g, **Saturated Fat** 1g, **Cholesterol** 0mg, **Sodium** 340mg, **Carbohydrates** 40g, **Dietary Fiber** 5g, **Protein** 5g

CAPRESE STUFFED ZUCCHINI BOATS

MAKES 6 SERVINGS

3 medium zucchini

1 package (3 ounces) ramen noodles, any flavor, broken into small pieces*

1 tomato, finely chopped

½ cup (2 ounces) shredded mozzarella cheese

2 tablespoons fresh chopped basil

1 tablespoon olive oil

1 clove garlic, minced

½ teaspoon salt

*Discard seasoning packet.

1. Slice zucchini in half lengthwise; scoop out seeds, leaving the shell. Cut off ends of zucchini or trim to fit in air fryer basket.

2. Cook ramen noodles in boiling water 2 minutes; drain and place in large bowl. Add tomato, cheese, basil, oil, garlic and salt; stir to combine. Divide mixture among shells.

3. Preheat air fryer to 350°F. Cook in batches 15 to 20 minutes or until zucchini is browned and noodles are lightly browned.

Calories 130, **Total Fat** 7g, **Saturated Fat** 2.5g, **Cholesterol** 5mg, **Sodium** 530mg, **Carbohydrates** 13g, **Dietary Fiber** 1g, **Protein** 5g

PARMESAN-CRUSTED FRENCH FRIES WITH ROSEMARY DIPPING SAUCE

MAKES 4 SERVINGS

3 medium baking potatoes (8 ounces each), peeled and cut into 12 wedges

1 tablespoon olive oil

⅛ teaspoon salt

⅛ teaspoon black pepper

¼ cup shredded Parmesan cheese

½ cup light mayonnaise

1 teaspoon chopped fresh rosemary *or* ½ teaspoon dried rosemary

½ teaspoon grated lemon peel

1 clove garlic, crushed

1. Preheat air fryer to 390°F. Toss potatoes with oil, salt and pepper in medium bowl.

2. Cook in batches 18 to 20 minutes, shaking halfway through cooking. Sprinkle cheese over potatoes. Cook additional 3 to 5 minutes until cheese melts and potatoes are tender.

3. Meanwhile, stir together mayonnaise, rosemary, lemon peel and garlic in small bowl. Serve potatoes with dipping sauce.

Calories 270, **Total Fat** 15g, **Saturated Fat** 3g, **Cholesterol** 15mg, **Sodium** 360mg, **Carbohydrates** 31g, **Dietary Fiber** 3g, **Protein** 5g

SAVORY STUFFED TOMATOES

MAKES 4 SERVINGS

2 large ripe tomatoes
(1 to 1¼ pounds total)

¾ cup garlic- or Caesar-
flavored croutons

¼ cup chopped pitted
kalamata olives
(optional)

2 tablespoons chopped
fresh basil

1 clove garlic, minced

2 tablespoons grated
Parmesan or Romano
cheese

1 tablespoon olive oil

1. Preheat air fryer to 350°F. Line basket with foil or parchment paper.

2. Cut tomatoes in half crosswise; discard seeds. Scrape out and reserve pulp. Set aside tomato shells.

3. Chop up tomato pulp; place in medium bowl. Add croutons, olives, basil and garlic; toss well. Spoon mixture into tomato shells. Sprinkle with cheese and drizzle oil over shells.

4. Cook 5 to 7 minutes or until heated through.

Calories 91, **Total Fat** 7g, **Saturated Fat** 1g, **Cholesterol** 3mg, **Sodium** 300mg, **Carbohydrates** 7g, **Dietary Fiber** 1g, **Protein** 4g

CRISPY FRIES WITH HERBED DIPPING SAUCE

MAKES 3 SERVINGS

Herbed Dipping Sauce
(recipe follows)

2 large unpeeled baking
potatoes

1 tablespoon vegetable
oil

½ teaspoon kosher salt

1. Prepare Herbed Dipping Sauce; set aside. Preheat air fryer to 390°F. Spray basket with nonstick cooking spray.

2. Cut potatoes into ¼-inch strips. Toss potato strips with oil in large bowl to coat evenly.

3. Cook in batches 18 to 20 minutes, shaking occasionally during cooking, until golden brown and crispy. Sprinkle with salt. Serve immediately with Herbed Dipping Sauce.

HERBED DIPPING SAUCE: Stir ¼ cup mayonnaise, 1 tablespoon chopped fresh herbs (such as basil, parsley, oregano and/or dill), ¼ teaspoon salt and ⅛ teaspoon black pepper in small bowl until smooth and well blended. Cover and refrigerate until ready to serve.

Calories 290, **Total Fat** 12g, **Saturated Fat** 1.5g, **Cholesterol** 5mg, **Sodium** 660mg, **Carbohydrates** 44g, **Dietary Fiber** 4g, **Protein** 4g

RICH ROASTED SESAME VEGETABLES

MAKES 2 SERVINGS

1 carrot, quartered lengthwise and cut into 2-inch pieces

1 medium sweet potato, peeled and cut into ¾-inch cubes

½ red bell pepper, cut into 1-inch cubes

½ medium onion, cut into ½-inch wedges

1 tablespoon dark sesame oil

2 teaspoons sugar

¼ teaspoon salt

1. Preheat air fryer to 390°F. Line basket with foil.

2. Place carrot, sweet potato, bell pepper and onion in large bowl. Sprinkle with oil, sugar and salt; toss gently to coat.

3. Cook 10 to 12 minutes, shaking occasionally during cooking, until vegetables are tender and browned.

TIP: Before serving, sprinkle vegetables with rice vinegar or lime juice.

Calories 165, **Total Fat** 7g, **Saturated Fat** 1g, **Cholesterol** 0mg, **Sodium** 346mg, **Carbohydrates** 25g, **Dietary Fiber** 4g, **Protein** 2g

ORANGE AND MAPLE-GLAZED ROASTED BEETS

MAKES 4 SERVINGS

4 medium beets, scrubbed

¼ cup orange juice

3 tablespoons balsamic or cider vinegar

2 tablespoons maple syrup

2 teaspoons grated orange peel, divided

1 teaspoon Dijon mustard

Salt and black pepper

1 to 2 tablespoons chopped fresh mint (optional)

1. Preheat air fryer to 390°F.

2. Peel and cut beets in half lengthwise; cut into wedges. Place in large bowl.

3. Whisk orange juice, vinegar, maple syrup, 1 teaspoon orange peel and mustard in small bowl until well blended. Pour half over beets.

4. Cook 22 to 25 minutes, shaking occasionally during cooking, until softened. Remove to serving dish; pour remaining orange juice mixture over beets. Season with salt and pepper. Sprinkle with remaining 1 teaspoon orange peel and mint, if desired.

Calories 100, **Total Fat** 3g, **Saturated Fat** 0g, **Cholesterol** 0mg, **Sodium** 100mg, **Carbohydrates** 19g, **Dietary Fiber** 2g, **Protein** 2g

CRUNCHY PARMESAN ZUCCHINI STICKS
(page 168)

CHAPTER 6

CHIPS & SNACKS

BUTTERNUT SQUASH OVEN CHIPS

MAKES 4 SERVINGS

Lime Yogurt Dip
(recipe follows)

½ teaspoon garlic powder

¼ teaspoon salt

¼ teaspoon ground red
pepper

1 butternut squash
(about 2½ pounds),
peeled, seeded and
cut crosswise into
3-inch thin slices

2 teaspoons vegetable oil

1. Preheat oven to 425°F. Prepare Lime Yogurt Dip. Combine garlic powder, salt and ground red pepper in small bowl.

2. Thinly slice butternut squash (or use spiral cutter with thick spiral blade to slice); place in large bowl. Drizzle with oil and sprinkle with seasoning mix; gently toss to coat.

3. Cook 18 to 20 minutes or until squash is browned and crisp, shaking occasionally during cooking. Serve with Lime Yogurt Dip.

LIME YOGURT DIP: Combine ¼ cup reduced-fat mayonnaise, ¼ cup reduced-fat Greek yogurt, 1 teaspoon lime juice and ¼ teaspoon grated lime peel in small bowl. Refrigerate until ready to serve.

Calories 190, **Total Fat** 8g, **Saturated Fat** 1g, **Cholesterol** 5mg, **Sodium** 260mg, **Carbohydrates** 32g, **Dietary Fiber** 5g, **Protein** 4g

SAVORY ZUCCHINI STIX

MAKES 4 SERVINGS

3 tablespoons seasoned dry bread crumbs

2 tablespoons grated Parmesan cheese

1 egg white

1 teaspoon reduced-fat (2%) milk

2 small zucchini (about 4 ounces each), cut lengthwise into quarters

⅓ cup pasta sauce, warmed

1. Preheat air fryer to 370°F. Spray basket with nonstick cooking spray.

2. Combine bread crumbs and Parmesan cheese in shallow dish. Combine egg white and milk in another shallow dish; beat with fork until well blended.

3. Dip each zucchini wedge into crumb mixture, then into egg white mixture, letting excess drip back into dish. Roll again in crumb mixture to coat. Spray zucchini with cooking spray.

4. Cook 12 to 14 minutes, shaking halfway during cooking, until golden brown. Serve with pasta sauce.

Calories 69, **Total Fat** 2g, **Saturated Fat** 1g, **Cholesterol** 6mg, **Sodium** 329mg, **Carbohydrates** 9g, **Dietary Fiber** 1g, **Protein** 4g

BITE-YOU-BACK ROASTED EDAMAME

MAKES 4 SERVINGS

2 teaspoons vegetable oil

2 teaspoons honey

¼ teaspoon wasabi powder*

1 package (about 12 ounces) shelled edamame, thawed if frozen

Kosher salt (optional)

Wasabi powder can be found in the Asian section of most supermarkets and in Asian specialty markets.

1. Preheat air fryer to 370°F.

2. Combine oil, honey and wasabi powder in large bowl; mix well. Add edamame; toss to coat.

3. Cook 12 to 14 minutes, shaking occasionally during cooking, until lightly browned. Remove from basket to large bowl; sprinkle generously with salt, if desired. Cool completely before serving. Store in airtight container.

Calories 120, **Total Fat** 6g, **Saturated Fat** 0g, **Cholesterol** 0mg, **Sodium** 5mg, **Carbohydrates** 9g, **Dietary Fiber** 4g, **Protein** 10g

KALE CHIPS

MAKES 6 SERVINGS

1 large bunch kale (about 1 pound)

1 tablespoon olive oil

1 teaspoon garlic powder

½ teaspoon salt

½ teaspoon black pepper

1. Preheat air fryer to 390°F.

2. Wash kale and pat dry with paper towels. Remove center ribs and stems; discard. Cut leaves into 2- to 3-inch-wide pieces.

3. Combine leaves, oil, garlic powder, salt and pepper in large bowl; toss to coat.

4. Cook in batches 3 to 4 minutes or until edges are lightly browned and leaves are crisp. Cool completely. Store in airtight container.

Calories 60, **Total Fat** 3g, **Saturated Fat** 0g, **Cholesterol** 0mg, **Sodium** 230mg, **Carbohydrates** 7g, **Dietary Fiber** 3g, **Protein** 3g

EGGPLANT NIBBLES

MAKES 4 SERVINGS

1 egg

1 tablespoon water

½ cup Italian-seasoned
  bread crumbs

1 Asian eggplant
  or 1 small globe
  eggplant

  Marinara sauce
  (optional)

1. Preheat air fryer to 370°F. Line basket with foil or parchment paper.

2. Beat egg and water in shallow dish. Place bread crumbs in another shallow dish.

3. Cut ends off of eggplant. Peel and cut into sticks about 3 inches long by ½-inch wide.

4. Coat eggplant sticks in egg, then roll in bread crumbs. Spray with olive oil cooking spray.

5. Cook 12 to 14 minutes, shaking occasionally during cooking, until eggplant is tender and lightly browned. Serve with marinara sauce, if desired.

Calories 100, **Total Fat** 2g, **Saturated Fat** 0.5g, **Cholesterol** 45mg, **Sodium** 220mg, **Carbohydrates** 17g, **Dietary Fiber** 3g, **Protein** 5g

CORN TORTILLA CHIPS

MAKES 6 DOZEN CHIPS (12 SERVINGS)

6 (6-inch) corn tortillas, preferably day-old

½ teaspoon salt

Prepared guacamole or salsa (optional)

1. If tortillas are fresh, let stand, uncovered, in single layer on wire rack 1 to 2 hours to dry slightly.

2. Stack tortillas; cut tortillas into 6 or 8 equal wedges. Spray tortillas generously with nonstick olive oil cooking spray.

3. Preheat air fryer to 370°F.

4. Cook in batches 5 to 6 minutes, shaking halfway through cooking. Sprinkle with salt. Serve with guacamole or salsa, if desired.

NOTE: Tortilla chips are served with salsa as a snack, used as the base for nachos and used as scoops for guacamole, other dips or refried beans. They are best eaten fresh, but can be stored, tightly covered, in a cool place 2 or 3 days.

Calories 30, **Total Fat** 0g, **Saturated Fat** 0g, **Cholesterol** 0mg, **Sodium** 100mg, **Carbohydrates** 6g, **Dietary Fiber** 0g, **Protein** 1g

ROASTED CHICKPEAS

MAKES 1 CUP (4 SERVINGS)

1 can (about 15 ounces) chickpeas, rinsed and drained

1 tablespoon olive oil

½ teaspoon salt

½ teaspoon black pepper

¼ tablespoon chili powder

¼ teaspoon ground red pepper

1 lime, cut into wedges (optional)

1. Preheat air fryer to 390°F.

2. Combine chickpeas, oil, salt and black pepper in large bowl.

3. Cook 8 to 10 minutes, shaking occasionally during cooking, until chickpeas begin to brown.

4. Sprinkle with chili powder and ground red pepper. Serve with lime wedges, if desired.

Calories 120, **Total Fat** 4.5g, **Saturated Fat** 0g, **Cholesterol** 0mg, **Sodium** 540mg, **Carbohydrates** 15g, **Dietary Fiber** 4g, **Protein** 4g

SPICY BAKED SWEET POTATO CHIPS

MAKES 4 SERVINGS

1 teaspoon sugar

½ teaspoon smoked paprika

¼ teaspoon salt

¼ teaspoon ground red pepper

2 medium sweet potatoes, unpeeled and cut into very thin slices

2 teaspoons vegetable oil

1. Preheat air fryer to 390°F. Combine sugar, paprika, salt and ground red pepper in small bowl; set aside.

2. Place potatoes in large bowl; drizzle with oil; toss to coat.

3. Cook in batches 12 to 14 minutes. Shake chips; sprinkle with seasoning mix. Cook 3 to 5 minutes, shaking frequently, until chips are lightly browned and crisp. Cool completely.

Calories 80, **Total Fat** 2.5g, **Saturated Fat** 0g, **Cholesterol** 0mg, **Sodium** 180mg, **Carbohydrates** 13g, **Dietary Fiber** 2g, **Protein** 1g

SAVORY PITA CHIPS

MAKES 4 SERVINGS

2 whole wheat or white pita bread rounds

3 tablespoons grated Parmesan cheese

1 teaspoon dried basil

¼ teaspoon garlic powder

1. Preheat air fryer to 350°F.

2. Carefully cut each pita round in half horizontally; split into two rounds. Cut each round into six wedges. Spray wedges with nonstick cooking spray.

3. Combine Parmesan, basil and garlic powder in small bowl; sprinkle evenly over pita wedges.

4. Cook 8 to 10 minutes, shaking occasionally during cooking, until golden brown. Cool completely.

CINNAMON CRISPS: Substitute butter-flavored cooking spray for olive oil cooking spray and 1 tablespoon sugar mixed with ¼ teaspoon ground cinnamon for Parmesan cheese, basil and garlic powder.

Calories 108, **Total Fat** 2g, **Saturated Fat** 1g, **Cholesterol** 4mg, **Sodium** 257mg, **Carbohydrates** 18g, **Dietary Fiber** 2g, **Protein** 5g

CRUNCHY PARMESAN ZUCCHINI STICKS

MAKES 6 SERVINGS

1 package (3 ounces) ramen noodles, any flavor

½ cup shredded Parmesan cheese

½ cup all-purpose flour

1 egg

1 tablespoon water

3 medium zucchini, cut into sticks

Prepared marinara sauce for dipping

1. Preheat air fryer to 390°F. Line basket with parchment paper; spray with nonstick cooking spray.

2. Place noodles and cheese in food processor; pulse until fine crumbs form. Pour into shallow dish.

3. Place flour and ramen seasoning packet in another shallow dish; stir to combine. Whisk egg and water in third shallow dish.

4. Dip zucchini sticks in flour mixture, then egg, then noodle mixture. Spray with cooking spray.

5. Cook in batches 12 to 15 minutes or until tender and golden brown. Serve warm with marinara sauce.

Calories 160, **Total Fat** 6g, **Saturated Fat** 2.5g, **Cholesterol** 35mg, **Sodium** 400mg, **Carbohydrates** 20g, **Dietary Fiber** 1g, **Protein** 7g

EASY WONTON CHIPS

MAKES 2 DOZEN CHIPS (4 SERVINGS)

1½ teapoons soy sauce

1 teaspoon peanut or vegetable oil

½ teaspoon sugar

¼ teaspoon garlic salt

12 wonton wrappers

1. Preheat air fryer to 370°F. Combine soy sauce, oil, sugar and garlic salt in small bowl; mix well.

2. Cut wonton wrappers diagonally in half. Spray with nonstick cooking spray. Brush soy sauce mixture lightly over both sides.

3. Cook in batches 3 to 5 minutes, shaking halfway through cooking, until crisp and lightly browned. Transfer to wire rack; cool completely.

Calories 80, **Total Fat** 1.5g, **Saturated Fat** 0g, **Cholesterol** 0mg, **Sodium** 400mg, **Carbohydrates** 15g, **Dietary Fiber** 0g, **Protein** 2g

SAUTÉED APPLES SUPREME
(page 178)

CHAPTER 7

SIMPLE SWEETS

PEACHES WITH RASPBERRY SAUCE

MAKES 4 SERVINGS

1 package (10 ounces) frozen raspberries, thawed

1½ teaspoons lemon juice

2 tablespoons packed brown sugar

½ teaspoon ground cinnamon

1 can (15 ounces) peach halves in juice (4 halves)

Foil

2 teaspoons butter, cut into small pieces

Fresh mint sprigs (optional)

1. Combine raspberries and lemon juice in food processor fitted with metal blade; process until smooth. Refrigerate until ready to serve.

2. Preheat air fryer to 350°F.

3. Combine brown sugar and cinnamon in medium bowl; coat peach halves with mixture. Place peach halves, cut sides up, on foil. Dot with butter. Fold foil over peaches. Place packet in basket.

4. Cook 6 to 8 minutes or until peaches are soft and lightly browned.

5. To serve, spoon 2 tablespoons raspberry sauce over each peach half. Garnish with mint.

Calories 120, **Total Fat** 2g, **Saturated Fat** 1g, **Cholesterol** 5mg, **Sodium** 5mg, **Carbohydrates** 28g, **Dietary Fiber** 5g, **Protein** 1g

PLUM-GINGER BRUSCHETTA

MAKES 9 SERVINGS

1 sheet frozen puff
   pastry (half of
   17¼-ounce package),
   thawed

2 cups chopped
   unpeeled firm ripe
   plums (about
   3 medium)

2 tablespoons sugar

2 tablespoons chopped
   candied ginger

1 tablespoon
   all-purpose flour

2 teaspoons lemon juice

⅛ teaspoon ground
   cinnamon

2 tablespoons apple
   jelly *or* apricot
   preserves

1. Preheat air fryer to 370°F. Line basket with parchment paper.

2. Cut puff pastry sheet lengthwise into 3 strips. Cut each strip crosswise in thirds to make 9 pieces. Cook in batches 5 to 6 minutes or until puffed and lightly browned.

3. Meanwhile, combine plums, sugar, ginger, flour, lemon juice and cinnamon in medium bowl.

4. Gently brush each puff pastry piece with about ½ teaspoon jelly; top with scant ¼ cup plum mixture. Cook in batches 1 to 2 minutes or until fruit is tender.

Calories 60, **Total Fat** 1.5g, **Saturated Fat** 0g, **Cholesterol** 0mg, **Sodium** 20mg, **Carbohydrates** 11g, **Dietary Fiber** 0g, **Protein** 1g

SAUTÉED APPLES SUPREME

MAKES 2 SERVINGS

2 small Granny Smith apples or 1 large Granny Smith apple

1 teaspoon butter, melted

2 tablespoons unsweetened apple juice or cider

1 teaspoon packed brown sugar

½ teaspoon ground cinnamon

⅔ cup vanilla ice cream or frozen yogurt (optional)

1 tablespoon chopped walnuts, toasted

1. Preheat air fryer to 350°F. Line basket with parchment paper; spray with nonstick cooking spray.

2. Cut apples into quarters; remove cores and cut into ½-inch-thick slices. Toss butter and apples in medium bowl.

3. Combine apple juice, brown sugar and cinnamon in small bowl; toss with apples.

4. Cook 6 to 8 minutes, shaking halfway through cooking, until soft and lightly golden. Transfer to serving bowls; serve with ice cream, if desired. Sprinkle with walnuts.

Calories 139, **Total Fat** 5g, **Saturated Fat** 2g, **Cholesterol** 6mg, **Sodium** 22mg, **Carbohydrates** 26g, **Dietary Fiber** 4g, **Protein** 1g

CHOCOLATE FRUIT TARTS

MAKES 6 TARTS

1 refrigerated pie crust (half of 15-ounce package)

1¼ cups prepared low-fat chocolate pudding (about 4 snack-size pudding cups)

Fresh sliced strawberries, raspberries, blackberries or favorite fruit

1. Preheat air fryer to 370°F. Spray 2½-inch silicone muffin cups with nonstick cooking spray. Unfold pie crust on lightly-floured surface. Let stand at room temperature 15 minutes.

2. Roll out pie crust on clean work surface; cut out six circles with 4-inch round cookie cutter. Place dough circles over backs of alternating muffin cups, pleating around sides of cups. (Press firmly to hold dough in place.) Prick bottom and sides with fork.

3. Cook in batches 8 to 10 minutes or until golden brown. Carefully remove tart shells from backs of muffin cups. Cool completely on wire rack.

4. Fill each tart shell with about 3 tablespoons pudding; arrange fruit on top.

Calories 240, **Total Fat** 9g, **Saturated Fat** 3.5g, **Cholesterol** 0mg, **Sodium** 260mg, **Carbohydrates** 37g, **Dietary Fiber** 1g, **Protein** 3g

ROASTED PLUMS WITH SPICED TOPPING

MAKES 4 SERVINGS

¼ cup toasted walnuts,* chopped

⅛ teaspoon ground cumin

⅛ teaspoon ground cinnamon

1 teaspoon ground ginger

4 red plums, pitted and cut in half

1 teaspoon olive oil

¼ cup crumbled Gorgonzola cheese

To toast walnuts, spread in single layer in heavy skillet. Cook over medium heat 3 minutes or until nuts are fragrant, stirring frequently.

1. Preheat air fryer to 350°F. Line basket with parchment paper.

2. Combine walnuts, cumin, cinnamon and ginger in small bowl; set aside.

3. Brush plums with oil. Cook, cut sides up, 6 to 8 minutes or until tender. Remove plums to serving plate.

4. Sprinkle with cheese and walnuts.

COOK'S TIP: What is a "pinch"? It is one-sixteenth of a teaspoon, about the amount of spices or herbs you can hold between your thumb and forefinger. In some gourmet shops, you can find pinch-, smidgen-, and dash-size measuring spoons.

Calories 77, **Total Fat** 4.5g, **Saturated Fat** 1g, **Cholesterol** 3mg, **Sodium** 48mg, **Carbohydrates** 8g, **Dietary Fiber** 1g, **Protein** 2g

YOGURT LIME TARTLETS

MAKES 8 TARTLETS

1 refrigerated pie crust (half of 15-ounce package)

1 cup plain nonfat Greek yogurt

2 tablespoons honey

1 egg, lightly beaten

Grated peel and juice of 1 lime

Additional grated lime peel (optional)

1. Preheat air fryer to 370°F. Unroll pie crust onto clean work surface. Cut out circles with 3-inch round cookie cutter. Re-roll scraps of dough to cut out total of eight circles. Press dough into bottoms and up sides of silicon muffin cups.

2. Stir yogurt, honey, egg, lime peel and lime juice in medium bowl until well blended. Spoon 1 tablespoon mixture into each muffin cup.

3. Cook 10 to 12 minutes or until filling is set and crust is golden brown. Cool 5 minutes. Remove to wire rack; cool completely. Refrigerate at least 2 hours before serving. Garnish with additional lime peel.

Calories 97, **Total Fat** 5g, **Saturated Fat** 2g, **Cholesterol** 13mg, **Sodium** 78mg, **Carbohydrates** 12g, **Dietary Fiber** 1g, **Protein** 2g

BAKED CINNAMON APPLES

MAKES 2 SERVINGS

2 large Granny Smith apples

2 sheets heavy-duty foil, lightly sprayed with nonstick cooking spray

2 tablespoons packed brown sugar

2 tablespoons dried cranberries

½ teaspoon ground cinnamon

2 teaspoons butter

Vanilla ice cream (optional)

1. Preheat air fryer to 350°F. Core apples. Using paring knife, trim off ½-inch strip around top of each apple. Place each apple in center of foil sheet.

2. Mix brown sugar, cranberries and cinnamon in small bowl. Fill inside of apples with sugar mixture, sprinkling any excess around pared rim. Place 1 teaspoon butter on sugar mixture on each apple; press gently.

3. Fold foil around apples. Place in basket.

4. Cook 12 to 14 minutes or until apples are slightly softened. Transfer apples to bowls; spoon remaining liquid over apples. Serve warm apples with ice cream, if desired.

Calories 240, **Total Fat** 4.5g, **Saturated Fat** 2.5g, **Cholesterol** 10mg, **Sodium** 5mg, **Carbohydrates** 50g, **Dietary Fiber** 7g, **Protein** 1g

CARAMELIZED PINEAPPLE

MAKES 4 SERVINGS

2 cups fresh pineapple chunks

1 tablespoon butter, melted

3 tablespoons packed brown sugar

¾ cup vanilla frozen yogurt or ice cream

1. Preheat air fryer to 350°F. Line basket with foil or parchment paper; spray with nonstick cooking spray.

2. Place pineapple in large bowl. Drizzle with butter; toss with brown sugar.

3. Cook 6 to 8 minutes or until golden brown, shaking occasionally during cooking.

4. Spoon pineapple into four dessert dishes. Top each evenly with frozen yogurt. Serve immediately.

Calories 145, **Total Fat** 4g, **Saturated Fat** 1g, **Cholesterol** 4mg, **Sodium** 52mg, **Carbohydrates** 28g, **Dietary Fiber** 1g, **Protein** 2g

INDEX

METRIC CONVERSION CHART

VOLUME MEASUREMENTS (dry)

$\frac{1}{8}$ teaspoon = 0.5 mL
$\frac{1}{4}$ teaspoon = 1 mL
$\frac{1}{2}$ teaspoon = 2 mL
$\frac{3}{4}$ teaspoon = 4 mL
1 teaspoon = 5 mL
1 tablespoon = 15 mL
2 tablespoons = 30 mL
$\frac{1}{4}$ cup = 60 mL
$\frac{1}{3}$ cup = 75 mL
$\frac{1}{2}$ cup = 125 mL
$\frac{2}{3}$ cup = 150 mL
$\frac{3}{4}$ cup = 175 mL
1 cup = 250 mL
2 cups = 1 pint = 500 mL
3 cups = 750 mL
4 cups = 1 quart = 1 L

VOLUME MEASUREMENTS (fluid)

1 fluid ounce (2 tablespoons) = 30 mL
4 fluid ounces ($\frac{1}{2}$ cup) = 125 mL
8 fluid ounces (1 cup) = 250 mL
12 fluid ounces (1$\frac{1}{2}$ cups) = 375 mL
16 fluid ounces (2 cups) = 500 mL

WEIGHTS (mass)

$\frac{1}{2}$ ounce = 15 g
1 ounce = 30 g
3 ounces = 90 g
4 ounces = 120 g
8 ounces = 225 g
10 ounces = 285 g
12 ounces = 360 g
16 ounces = 1 pound = 450 g

DIMENSIONS

$\frac{1}{16}$ inch = 2 mm
$\frac{1}{8}$ inch = 3 mm
$\frac{1}{4}$ inch = 6 mm
$\frac{1}{2}$ inch = 1.5 cm
$\frac{3}{4}$ inch = 2 cm
1 inch = 2.5 cm

OVEN TEMPERATURES

250°F = 120°C
275°F = 140°C
300°F = 150°C
325°F = 160°C
350°F = 180°C
375°F = 190°C
400°F = 200°C
425°F = 220°C
450°F = 230°C

BAKING PAN SIZES

Utensil	Size in Inches/Quarts	Metric Volume	Size in Centimeters
Baking or Cake Pan (square or rectangular)	8×8×2	2 L	20×20×5
	9×9×2	2.5 L	23×23×5
	12×8×2	3 L	30×20×5
	13×9×2	3.5 L	33×23×5
Loaf Pan	8×4×3	1.5 L	20×10×7
	9×5×3	2 L	23×13×7
Round Layer Cake Pan	8×1½	1.2 L	20×4
	9×1½	1.5 L	23×4
Pie Plate	8×1¼	750 mL	20×3
	9×1¼	1 L	23×3
Baking Dish or Casserole	1 quart	1 L	—
	1½ quart	1.5 L	—
	2 quart	2 L	—